CURIOUS
CREATURES
of Australia

Doug Priestly

PUFFIN BOOKS

To my father, Des.
Thanks for believing.

Puffin Books
Penguin Books Australia Ltd
487 Maroondah Highway, PO Box 257
Ringwood, Victoria 3134, Australia
Penguin Books Ltd, Harmondsworth, Middlesex, England
Viking Penguin, A Division of Penguin Books USA Inc.
375 Hudson Street, New York, New York 10014, USA
Penguin Books Canada Limited
10 Alcorn Avenue, Toronto, Ontario, Canada M4V 3B2
Penguin Books (N.Z.) Ltd
182-190 Wairau Road, Auckland 10, New Zealand

First published by Penguin Books Australia, 1995
3 5 7 9 10 8 6 4 2
Copyright © Doug Priestly, 1995

Typeset in Bembo
Made and printed in Hong Kong through Bookbuilders Ltd

National Library of Australia
Cataloguing-in-Publication data:
Priestly, Doug
Curious creatures of Australia
ISBN 0 14 055347 9
1. Zoology - Australia - Pictorial works - Juvenile literature.
I. Title. (Series: Picture Puffin fact books).
591.994

The illustrations in this book were executed
in watercolour and gouache.

Contents

Introduction 4

Thorny Devil 5

Leafy Sea Dragon 6

Underground Orchid 7

Tawny Frogmouth 8

Honeypot Ants 9

Magnificent Spider 10

Western Australian Pitcher Plant 11

Blind Cave Fish 12

Blue-ringed Octopus 13

Mudskipper 14

Gastric-brooding Frog 15

Catbird 16

Leaf-tailed Gecko 17

Nurseryfish 18

Turtle Frog 19

Marsupial Mole 20

Insect-imitating Orchid 21

Stonefish 22

Imperial Blue Butterfly 23

Bilby 24

Water-holding Frog 25

Lungfish 26

Striped Possum 27

Archerfish 28

Hip-pocket Frog 29

Satin Bowerbird 30

Red Triangle Slug 31

Glossary 32

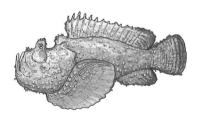

Introduction

Most people have heard of the platypus, but how many have actually seen one in the wild? Did you know that the male platypus has poisonous spurs on its hind feet? No? Australia is home to many strange and interesting plants and animals besides the well-known platypus. Would you believe there is a plant that grows and flowers completely underground? Or how about a frog that carries its young around in special 'hip pockets'? Have you ever seen a tawny frogmouth?

platypus
up to 60cm long

These are just a few of the oddities you will meet in this book. Living on land and in water, in deserts and in rainforests, in rivers and on coral reefs, they may seem weird to us, but their habits and appearances are all designed for one purpose - survival. You might see some of these creatures in your city or suburb. Others are very rare and are only found in remote areas of our vast continent. One creature, the gastric-brooding frog, may even be extinct. Turn the pages now and discover the amazing secrets of *Curious Creatures of Australia*.

With a spiky body and horned head, this little lizard certainly looks like some kind of 'devil'. It's quite harmless however, and is only dangerous to the ants it feeds upon - up to one thousand or more in a single meal! The thorny devil is well adapted to life in a desert environment and has an amazing way of taking a drink.

thorny devil
15-20cm long

Thorny Devil

This clever lizard only needs to touch a dew-covered bush or puddle of water with any part of its body and *hey presto!* - moisture is quickly drawn up along microscopic grooves in its rough skin to its mouth! A mottled colour pattern helps to disguise the thorny devil against predators, although it is hard to imagine any creature enjoying such a prickly meal!

5

Leafy Sea Dragon

No fierce, fire-breathing dragon is this, but a gentle member of the seahorse family. This dainty creature has evolved a wonderful disguise to fool predators. Leafy growths all along its body make it look like a piece of seaweed drifting along in the ocean. It's rather like the torn and tattered sails of some ghostly galleon, don't you think? The leafy sea dragon is found in rocky, coastal waters off southern Australia, especially where kelp (a type of seaweed) grows.

'baby' sea dragon

leafy sea dragon
up to 30cm long

Notice the tube-like mouth? It uses this to pluck tiny crustaceans and worms from its surroundings. The male leafy sea dragon is a good mother. After mating with the female, he takes care of the eggs, carrying them around under his tail until they hatch. Delightful baby 'dragons'!

This little orchid is one of the world's most unusual plants. It grows and flowers entirely underground. Without roots or leaves to take up nutrients and lacking chlorophyll (green pigment) for photosynthesis, how does it survive? By robbery and murder, that's how! The underground orchid is always found living close to the roots of a shrub called broombush. A kind of fungus living within the orchid's cells sends out fine threads through the soil to surround the roots of the broombush.

underground orchid
flower up to 2.5cm across
flower and stem up to 5cm in height

The fungus takes nutrients from these roots and transfers them back to the orchid. The greedy orchid then kills off the fungus and steals the nutrients for itself. The sweet-scented pink and maroon flowers attract tiny flies, ants and termites that crawl down through cracks in the soil. These insects pollinate the orchid flowers.

flower from above

Underground Orchid

Creatures such as frogs, mice and spiders are snapped up in its huge bill and *munch! crunch! gulp!* – down they go! You can see how it got its common name. The tawny frogmouth is found in the suburbs as well as country areas throughout most of Australia. Although often mistaken for an owl, this curious bird does not belong to the owl family. One difference is that the tawny frogmouth always catches its prey with its beak whereas owls use their hawk-like talons for hunting.

tawny frogmouth
up to 50cm long

You could walk right past this quiet forest dweller without ever knowing. During the daytime, the frogmouth sits motionless, with eyes closed and body held upright. Having a finely mottled pattern of grey, white and brown, the crafty frogmouth would have you believe it's a dead branch or tree limb. When night falls, this bird hunts from a low perch, swooping down silently on unsuspecting prey.

Tawny Frogmouth

8

These honeypot ants can hardly move! They spend their time hanging in clusters from the roof of the nest. When food becomes scarce above ground, nectar is taken from them by other workers and in this way the ant colony can survive till better times. Once empty, the honeypot workers return to their original size. Aborigines regard these ants as great bush tucker.

Honeypot Ants

honeypot ants
2-2.5cm long
when filled with nectar

Honeypot ants live in tunnels beneath the arid scrubland of central Australia and are masters of the art of survival in this often harsh landscape. Summer rains cause the desert shrubs to grow and flower. It is a time of plenty and the flowers are laden with sweet nectar which the worker ants gather busily. Back at the nest, certain other workers are fed such large amounts of this nectar that their abdomens swell to bursting point.

honeypot worker ant
1-1.5cm long

The female magnificent spider has a very unusual way of catching her dinner. She spins a 'fishing line' of silk and 'baits' it with special droplets of the same silk. These droplets contain a scent that certain male moths find irresistible! At night the spider dangles her line and waits for a moth to approach. When a moth flutters into range, the spider twirls the line around and tries to hit it. If the moth comes too close - *splat!* - the droplets burst and cover it in sticky silk.

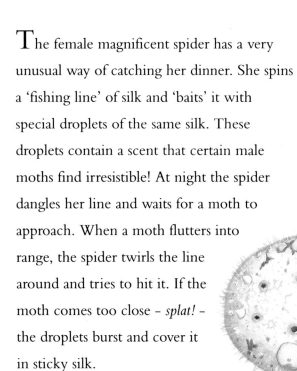

magnificent spider
10–12mm across,
not including legs

Magnificent Spider

The moth is trapped and the spider then 'reels' in her catch. I wonder, though, if the magnificent spider gets tired of having moths for dinner every night. Although we know a lot about the female, very little is known about the habits of the tiny male magnificent spider.

Carnivorous plants are often found growing in sandy, swampy ground, poor in nutrients needed for proper plant growth (especially nitrogen). Over time, they have evolved various ways of capturing and digesting insects and other creatures to supplement their 'diets'. Plants need their vitamins too! As well as having normal, oval-shaped leaves, the Western Australian pitcher plant has special, pouch-like leaves called pitchers.

cross-section of pitcher showing ant in digestive fluid

These have a lid and a ribbed mouth leading down into the pitcher. Ants and other insects are attracted by nectar glands on the outside of the pitchers. Here they are safe, but once inside there is no escape! The inner walls of the pitcher are slippery, and spikes pointing downwards force the unlucky insects into the digestive fluid below. They drown and are broken down by enzymes in the liquid to become part of the plant.

pitcher plant
up to 5cm in height

Western Australian Pitcher Plant

organs, called papillae, on the fishes' bodies tell them when food animals are near enough to catch. Like many creatures that live underground, their eyes have completely disappeared. These fascinating fish are only found in flooded limestone caves and tunnels in a dry, rocky corner of north-western Australia.

blind eel up to 35cm long

blind gudgeon up to 5cm long

Just imagine if you lived in constant darkness... How would you find your way around? Or find food? Your eyes would be no use at all. You would have to rely on your other senses to survive. And that's exactly what these two kinds of cave-dwelling fish do. The long, slender blind eel and the smaller blind gudgeon use their keen sense of touch to locate prey, such as mosquito wrigglers and small crustaceans. Tiny hair-like sense

Blind Cave Fish

Blue-ringed Octopus

The difference is two large venom glands located near this little beast's mouth. When bitten, the victim is injected with toxin that causes paralysis in five to ten minutes. It can be fatal, even to humans. Normally the blue-ringed octopus uses this toxin to immobilise crabs, its favourite food. There are two kinds of blue-ringed octopus found in Australia. The larger one lives along the northern coastline, the smaller one around our southern shores.

blue-ringed octopus
up to 20cm across,
including legs

Sometimes found in old tin cans or under rocks in shallow water, the blue-ringed octopus looks harmless enough. Don't be fooled though. This creature has a deadly bite. When handled or afraid, it darkens in colour and those blue rings become bigger, brighter and more iridescent. They're telling you, 'Leave me alone, I'm dangerous!' Like other octopuses, the blue-ringed octopus has a mouth rather like a parrot's beak.

Mudskipper

The comical mudskipper looks as though it couldn't decide whether to be a frog or a fish. It is definitely a fish, however - one that has learned to live and breathe out of water. Before venturing onto land, the mudskipper fills its gill chambers with water, returning regularly to get a fresh supply. It extracts oxygen from this water but can also breathe through its skin! Once on land, the mudskipper crawls about with the help of strong front fins and can jump swiftly if danger threatens.

mudskipper
9-10cm long

Those bulging eyes alert the fish to any enemy, such as a hungry heron that might want it for lunch. Mudskippers can be found living in mangrove swamps and mudflats along the northern coast of Australia.

14

Dwelling in cool, rocky rainforest creeks in south-eastern Queensland, the female gastric-brooding frog has a unique way of rearing her young. After laying her eggs, she swallows them! The eggs are safe, though. They produce a special substance that stops the digestive juices in the mother's stomach from dissolving them. First the eggs change into tadpoles and then into baby frogs. How do the froglets get out? Through their mother's mouth! A medicine has been developed from the chemical formula released by the eggs. This is used to help heal people who have stomach ulcers.

gastric-brooding frog
up to 5.5cm long

The gastric-brooding frog shows us that even small, seemingly unimportant creatures can benefit mankind. This is why we need to preserve natural environments as much as possible. Unfortunately this little frog may already be extinct. None has been found since 1980.

Gastric-brooding Frog

Catbird

Nests are usually made high above the ground in thick vines or slender tree forks. Should a predator such as a python threaten the nestlings, one of the adult catbirds will pretend to have a broken wing and flutter around helplessly to lure the snake away from the nest. Clever catbird!

catbird
up to 30cm long

Take a walk through a rainforest in eastern Australia and you may hear a peculiar sound. Is that a baby crying or maybe a cat miaowing? Would you believe it's a bird? A catbird? No, I'm not kidding! Look high up in the forest canopy and you may see the green catbird calling to advertise its territory during the nesting season. Although the catbird belongs to the bowerbird family, it does not build a bower for mating display as both male and female catbirds build the nest and feed and protect their young.

catbird nest with babies

16

The gecko escapes while the attacker is fooled by the wriggling tail. A new one soon grows back though, usually smaller and less pointed than the old tail. Amongst the largest of Australia's geckos, the leaf-tailed gecko is surely one of the strangest.

leaf-tailed gecko
up to 20cm long

Night is the time to look for this spiny lizard. You'll need sharp eyes though. With a blotchy colour pattern and flattened body, it's almost invisible. The leaf-tailed gecko prowls along tree trunks and over rocks in its rainforest habitat, looking for spiders and other small prey. Sharp claws give it a good grip on bark and other rough surfaces. Like most geckos and many other lizards, the leaf-tailed gecko has a neat trick if attacked by an enemy. It leaves its tail behind!

Leaf-tailed Gecko

You're a fish, you've just mated and laid your eggs. How do you protect them? You carry them around on your head, that's how! At least that's what the male nurseryfish does. Once the female nurseryfish has laid her eggs, which look like a tiny bunch of grapes, the male picks them up with a bony hook high on his forehead. As he swims around, the eggs are bathed in a flow of oxygen-rich water and kept free of dirt and bacteria at the same time.

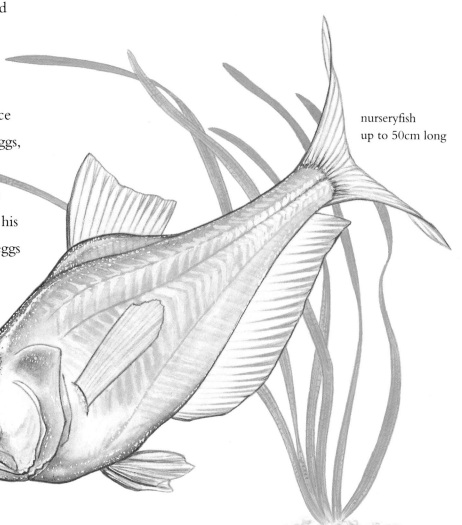

nurseryfish
up to 50cm long

Nurseryfish

'bunch' of eggs

Safe from other fish, the eggs develop *above* the watchful eyes of the devoted father. Also known as the humphead, the silvery-purple nurseryfish inhabits muddy rivers in tropical northern Australia, feeding on small fish, shrimp and other crustaceans.

Could this odd-looking creature really be a frog? It sure is! Probably the most unusual of Australia's frogs, the shy turtle frog spends most of its time underground. With strong forelegs it burrows headfirst into termite mounds and feasts on the termites within. It can gulp down hundreds of them in one meal! The turtle frog even breeds underground.

Turtle Frog

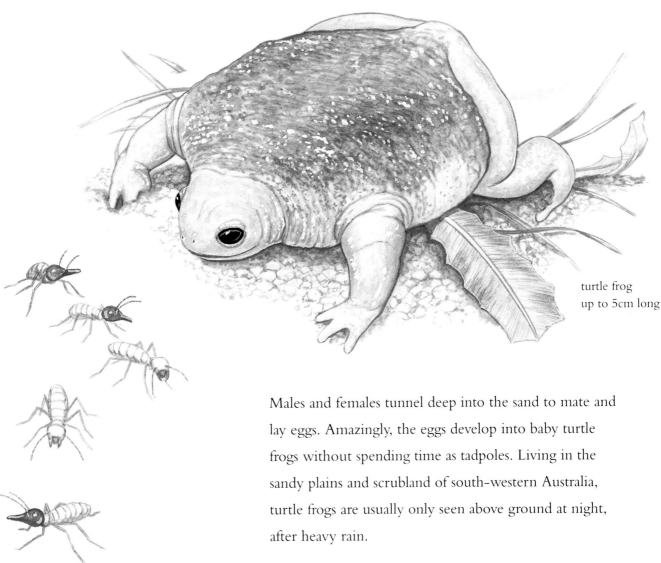

turtle frog
up to 5cm long

Males and females tunnel deep into the sand to mate and lay eggs. Amazingly, the eggs develop into baby turtle frogs without spending time as tadpoles. Living in the sandy plains and scrubland of south-western Australia, turtle frogs are usually only seen above ground at night, after heavy rain.

side view of mole

Little is known about the lifestyle or habits of this desert dweller but the female mole has a pouch for her young, like other marsupials. Not often seen above ground except after rain, the marsupial mole spends most of its time busily tunnelling through the sand. The mole hungrily devours insects and worms, in fact most smaller creatures it comes across. Watch out, lizard!

marsupial mole
up to 18cm long

Swim through sand? You've got to be joking! Yet that's just what this strange little animal seems to do. A beautiful golden or orange-yellow in colour, the marsupial mole is well equipped for living beneath the desert sands of central Australia. As the mole burrows forward with large, flattened front claws and a tough shielded snout, the sand fills in behind it. The marsupial mole is also completely blind and like many creatures adapted to living in darkness, its eyes have all but disappeared. No worries about getting sand in them!

Marsupial Mole

Insect-imitating Orchid

The male wasps fly off to investigate another tongue orchid flower, which is then fertilised by the pollen carried on their bodies. In this way, the tongue orchids are able to set seed and reproduce themselves.

Smart orchid, silly wasp!

orchid flower
up to 2.5cm in height by 3.5–4cm across
flower and stem up to 40cm in height

Who would have thought that a plant could outsmart an insect? The tricky tongue orchid can! This plant is one of a number of Australian orchids that pollinate their flowers by imitating the scent and shape of various female wasps, ants and flies. Male Ichneumon (*ick-new-mon*) wasps mistake the pink-purple flower of the tongue orchid for a female of their kind. Attracted by the flower's wasp-like smell, they try to mate with it. As they do, pollen gets stuck to the wasps' bodies.

*pollen grains stuck to
wasp's abdomen*

Stonefish

Is this the ugliest fish in the world? It is certainly the most venomous (poisonous). The stonefish is a poor swimmer and prefers to lie half-buried on the sea floor, waiting for a small fish or shrimp to pass within gulping range of its large mouth. Slimy and lumpy, the stonefish's body attracts sand, mud and algae that disguise it perfectly as a rock or piece of old coral. It's fun to watch

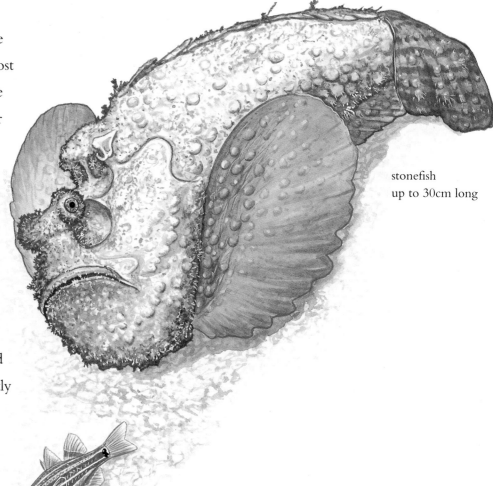

stonefish
up to 30cm long

stonefish in public aquariums, their fat white bellies wobbling as they paddle along. Stonefish are serious fish though. If disturbed or trodden on they have a deadly defence. Thirteen spines on the dorsal fin can inject the intruder with venom, just like a needle! Sometimes fatal to humans and other animals, the venom causes awful pain and sickness. If you're wading in the sea along Australia's northern shores, wear sandshoes and tread carefully.

side view of stonefish

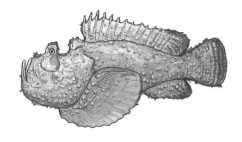

22

Fancy getting ants to look after your babies! The imperial blue butterfly does. The female lays her eggs on small wattle bushes and when the caterpillars emerge, each one finds itself surrounded by a 'bodyguard' of small, black ants. The ants 'shepherd' the brownish-black caterpillars as they move about the wattles to feed on the leaves.

If a wasp, spider or other predator tries to attack a caterpillar, the ants fiercely defend their helpless companions.

imperial blue butterfly
3-5cm across

view of upper wings showing blue colour

The caterpillar gains protection from enemies but what do the ants get in return? Would you believe, their sweets? Using their antennae, the ants continually stroke the body of the caterpillar causing it to exude a sugary substance that the ants find very tasty. As a result of this strange partnership, many more caterpillars survive to become imperial blue butterflies and the black ants gain a convenient food supply.

Imperial Blue Butterfly

Seeds and native fruits are taken from the soil surface, while the bilby uses its strong front claws to dig up plant bulbs and tubers below ground. Insects and small lizards are eaten as well. Conservationists are now trying to save the bilby from extinction by captive breeding and restoring some of its former habitat. Let's hope they succeed.

bilby
up to 90cm long,
including tail

Bilby

Wearing silky-soft, blue-grey fur and having ears that look a few sizes too big, the beautiful bilby is a charming creature. It's also one of our most endangered animals. A member of the bandicoot family, the bilby once occurred over most of Australia. Rabbits, cattle and sheep competing for food and living space, as well as feral predators such as cats and foxes, have slowly driven the bilby into a few remote desert areas. During the heat of the day, the bilby shelters in a burrow. Come night time, it is out and about foraging for food.

Water-holding Frog

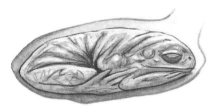

frog dormant in burrow

After heavy rain, the water-holding frog crawls out of the burrow to feed and breed. Eggs are laid in temporary pools and, once hatched out, the tadpoles race against time to grow and change into frogs before the pools dry up and the summer heat returns.

Did you know that some frogs live in the desert? One species called the water-holding frog has a smart way to beat the hot, dry conditions. It burrows underground and sheds its old skin to form a protective layer around itself. Just like a sleeping bag for frogs! This stops the frog from drying out while waiting dormant (sleeping) until the wet season begins. Water is also stored in the frog's bladder. During this time, the frog does not eat but instead uses its body fat for nourishment.

water-holding frog
4-6cm long

Lungfish

A relic of ancient times, the remarkable lungfish has remained almost unchanged since the age of the dinosaurs. It's truly a living fossil. Found only in a few rivers and dams in south-east Queensland, this primitive fish is mostly active at night. It seeks out frogs, tadpoles, fish and crustaceans, grinding them up in its curious comb-shaped teeth. The lungfish even likes a bit of salad now and then - it eats waterplants. You're probably asking yourself, 'Why is it called a lungfish?' Simple! During drought, when the water level is low and oxygen is scarce, instead of using its gills to breathe, the lungfish can gulp mouthfuls of air at the surface and take in oxygen through a special lung within its body. Although the lungfish of today grows quite large, in prehistoric Australia when most of the land was covered in rainforest, giant lungfish - three to four metres long - cruised the rivers and lagoons.

lungfish
up to 1.8m long

Moving like a black and white blur, the striped possum scurries along a branch, stopping every now and then to tap the bark with its front paw. What is it doing? If you said, 'looking for food', you'd be right. A hollow sound might mean there's a fat juicy beetle grub or moth larva hiding in a hole beneath the bark. Once found, the grub is prised out with the possum's elongated fourth finger and noisily eaten.

striped possum up to 60cm long, including tail

The striped possum not only looks a bit like the skunk of North America, it also has its own strong smell! The daylight hours are spent curled up in a leafy tree hollow and only at night will you see this possum, one of the most striking inhabitants of the tropical north Queensland rainforest.

elongated fourth finger

Striped Possum

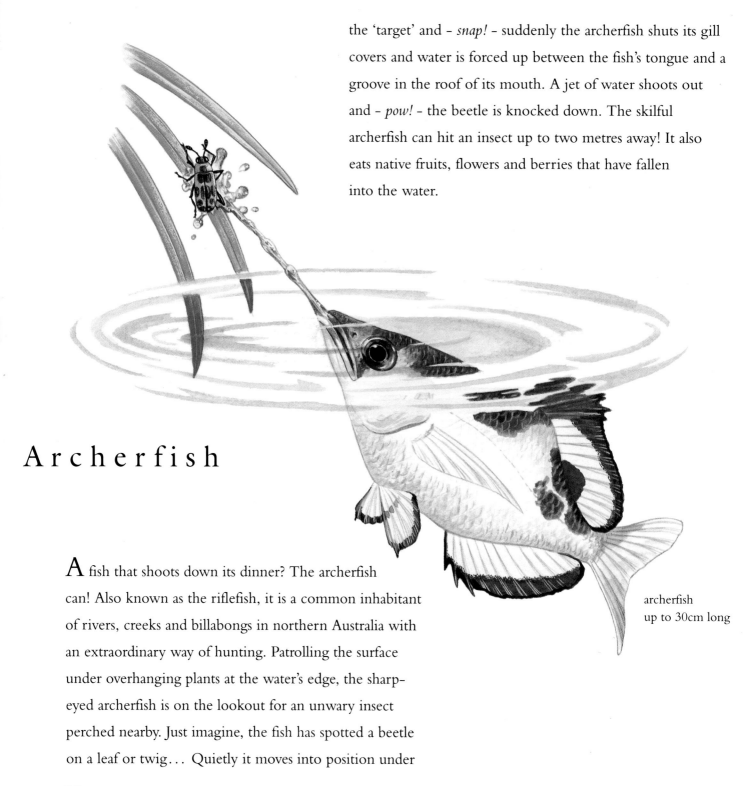

the 'target' and – *snap!* – suddenly the archerfish shuts its gill covers and water is forced up between the fish's tongue and a groove in the roof of its mouth. A jet of water shoots out and – *pow!* – the beetle is knocked down. The skilful archerfish can hit an insect up to two metres away! It also eats native fruits, flowers and berries that have fallen into the water.

Archerfish

A fish that shoots down its dinner? The archerfish can! Also known as the riflefish, it is a common inhabitant of rivers, creeks and billabongs in northern Australia with an extraordinary way of hunting. Patrolling the surface under overhanging plants at the water's edge, the sharp-eyed archerfish is on the lookout for an unwary insect perched nearby. Just imagine, the fish has spotted a beetle on a leaf or twig… Quietly it moves into position under

archerfish
up to 30cm long

28

Hip-pocket Frog

the tadpoles in, just like a kangaroo with a joey in her pouch. In fact, this tiny frog is also known as the marsupial frog. After about ten weeks, baby frogs climb out of the father's pockets, ready to explore their new home in the rainforest of south-eastern Queensland and northern New South Wales.

Male hip-pocket frogs like to keep a close eye on their young. They carry them wherever they go! Once eggs have been laid by the female frog, amongst damp soil and leaves on the forest floor, the male watches over them until they hatch. As the slippery white tadpoles leave the eggs, the male hip-pocket frog backs into the clump of spawn. *Squelch!* The tadpoles instinctively wriggle over their father's body until they find a small slit on either side of his stomach. Guess what happens then? They slither inside! The slits are the entrance to special pockets, one on either side of the male frog's body, that he uses to carry

hip-pocket frog
up to 2cm long

Satin Bowerbird

Think of your favourite colour. Is it blue? The male satin bowerbird is mad about blue. He builds a structure of sticks, called a bower, in order to attract and mate with female bowerbirds. The bower is then decorated with blue objects that take his fancy. Feathers, flowers, berries, bottle tops, pens, clothes pegs, drink straws and even small toys – anything blue! When a female approaches, the male satin bowerbird flashes his wings out and dances, purple eyes bulging with excitement and calling his harsh song.

satin bowerbird
up to 27cm long

Once the female bowerbird is enticed into the bower, the male mates with her. She then flies off to build a nest and raise her young all by herself. In the meantime, the male satin bowerbird busies himself with tidying and rearranging his bower until another female comes along. What a life!

What's the difference between a snail and a slug? A slug is simply a snail without a shell. In this case, a rather colourful one, don't you agree? This brilliant red slug is one of the many colour varieties of the wide-ranging red triangle slug that occurs in forest areas along much of Australia's eastern coast. Normally the slug is greyish with a red line around its edge and a red triangular patch on its back.

red triangle slug
(brilliant red colour variation)
up to 15cm when extended

However, in different areas you can find ones coloured rose-pink, yellow, gold, orange, even almost black. The bright red variety illustrated here is only found in a small national park in New South Wales. It lives in damp gullies and feeds on algae and lichen that it scrapes off rocks and logs with its file-like teeth. Notice the hole on the slug's back? That's a breathing hole connected to a simple lung within the slug's body. Who said slugs and snails were dull and boring!

red triangle slug
(normal colouring)

Red Triangle Slug

Glossary

abdomen   rear third section of an insect's body

antennae   the pair of hair-like sense organs on an insect's head

bacteria   single-celled microscopic life forms, neither plant nor animal, responsible for decay and some diseases

crustaceans   aquatic animals with a hard shell and two pairs of antennae, for example, the yabbie

environment   the kind of area a plant or animal lives in

enticed   lured or attracted

enzymes   natural chemicals produced by plants or animals for digestion and other life processes

feral   non-native animals roaming wild

gastric   to do with the stomach

iridescent   sparkling, rainbow-like colour

lichen   small plants which grow on the surface of rocks and trees

marsupial   a mammal that rears its young in a pouch

microscopic   able to be seen only with a microscope

nutrients   substances needed for plant or animal growth

photosynthesis   process by which plants turn sunlight into food, using chlorophyll (green pigment)

pollinate   to carry pollen for fertilisation

primitive   at an early stage of development

relic   something left over from another time

toxin   poison produced by a plant or animal

tubers   swollen underground plant stems or bulbs